GENTLY BETWEEN THE WORDS

Essays and Poems

ANDREW TAYLOR-TROUTMAN

FOREWORD BY APRIL WILLIAMS

Durham, NC

Copyright © 2019 Andrew Taylor-Troutman

Gently Between the Words: Essays and Poems
Andrew Taylor-Troutman
www.facebook.com/ataylortroutman
taylortroutman@yahoo.com

Published 2019, by Torchflame Books
An Imprint of Light Messages Publishing
www.lightmessages.com
SAN: 920-9298

Paperback ISBN: 978-1-61153-338-5
E-book ISBN: 978-1-61153-339-2
Library of Congress Control Number: 9781611533385

For Asa, our healer

CONTENTS

FOREWORD

The book you are holding, Andrew's book, is a gift. It will give different things to different people, but here is what it has given to me, his editor and friend.

Andrew's book has given me a better ability to appreciate beauty in my own life, what I have come to think of as "presence with perspective."

When Andrew asked me to edit his manuscript, I didn't know him at all. Of course, the first thing you do when you are contacted by someone out of the blue is to stalk that person on Facebook. I saw that Andrew and I had several friends in common, from random parts of my life—who knew? Our stories, it seems, are quite similar: We are the same age, have lived and currently live in similar places, have similar backgrounds, and are raising children of similar ages.

Needless to say, the stories Andrew shares in this book resonate with me on many levels. When he writes of cleaning up spilled milk with toilet paper while one child screams and another gleefully dumps Cheerios from the box, I can relate.

But being immersed in Andrew's writing, working regularly with the gentleness of his words, has imparted me with a life-altering perspective. I have found lately that when I am in the middle of the everyday storms of my life—of raising kids, of nurturing a marriage, of being an imperfect daughter, of suffering loss, and of joy so intense I immediately fear it will be fleeting—I'll catch myself thinking, "How would I write this story?"

How would I tell it like Andrew tells his stories, in ways that deliberately and thoughtfully find the beauty in it?

Having this thought flit through my mind in those big-feeling moments has graced me with perspective even while I am still right in the middle of the raging realities. It doesn't make the challenging times go away, but it gives me enough distance to breathe a tad easier and appreciate the moment *in* the moment, even if just a little. I liken it to meditation, but without having to sit up straight or focus on my breathing.

Over the past six months, Andrew and I have together pondered this word "beautiful." It is a word we wanted to pay attention to, particularly because we both have young daughters. I want to be aware of what I'm teaching my children about this very important but very loaded word. Andrew and I have dialogued about what "beautiful" means, how to use it, and when to use it, particularly with our girls.

Because of these talks, and dwelling in Andrew's book, I realize I think of beauty in terms of joy, appreciation, and gratitude.

I think for me, beauty is something that has very little to do with aesthetics and everything to do with my frame of mind. What I value as beautiful—what I hope to teach my daughter and son is beautiful—are the things that give joy. Not necessarily happiness, but joy—that deep, visceral, beyond-all-the-words feeling of appreciation and intense gratitude.

Andrew's book, in this way, is beautiful. It inspires me to see beauty amid the times that feel oh-so-unbeautiful, to seek out beauty when it is hard to see readily, and to appreciate it deeply when I do see it in the day-to-day ordinariness of my life. It helps me to be present with perspective—to appreciate the story of my life, as it is happening, as I am in the middle of all its messiness and wonder and heartbreak and joy.

Thank you, Andrew, for this beautiful gift.

And to you, Andrew's reader, I'm excited for you, because beauty and humor and gentleness and wisdom await you in the pages ahead. I hope you enjoy them as much as I have.

April Williams
Saxapahaw, North Carolina

PREFACE: WHEN WE DO NOT HAVE THE WORDS

... and we think that we can't
Write that for which we do not have words
but actually
Sometimes you can if you go
gently between the words.
—Brian Doyle

April Williams wrote the gracious foreword to this book. Throughout the revision process, she also made it crystal clear when my words did not resonate with her. One of the essays, the heartfelt letter I write to my daughter, was at one time titled "Nostrils." I'm glad she turned up her nose at that title!

But "Gently Between the Words" was my very first title for this book. This phrase is from a poem Brian Doyle wrote about his young daughter, and eventually I circled back to this enigmatic idea of Brian's. I find the phrase hard to explain. I love the poetic ring to it.

"Gently between the words" is figurative language, so it shouldn't be interpreted as having only one meaning, like an answer to an equation or a single verdict in a trial. To me, the phrase's meaning has to do with a probing curiosity—a reader seeking to find a personal connection with the author's description. That's what Brian Doyle's words have meant to me. He was my mentor and friend.

I learned from Brian's book *Spirited Men* that the ancient Greek biographer Plutarch wrote about the great men and women of his time in order to discover models of virtue for his own life. In other words, Plutarch wrote biographies as moral catechisms—each was a study of a life that read like a sermon. Brian ends his own essay on Plutarch by imagining the biographer's young daughter interrupting her father's work, begging him to take a walk with her down the beach. According to Doyle's imagination, this great moral philosopher of antiquity halted his sermonizing, "And he says 'yes of course my tiny flower' and down the street they go to the sea, father and daughter, hand in hand, immortal."

I think *that* is a darn good sermon.

"A father and daughter, hand in hand, immortal." These ringing words reinforce for me that if we glimpse any of the everlasting, it is in the moment. If we catch any vision of universality, it is in the particular. When we think we do not have the words, for certain moments in life seem too much to describe, we can still write in hopes of honoring those moments with a language that falls into step with our feelings and walks in the same direction, heart and mind.

I confess that I should be better with finding the right titles. Sermons have been a part of my life for as long as I can remember, for I grew up as a preacher's kid, and now I preach every Sunday. I find it hard to find time to craft the perfect title because I'm married to a preacher and we have three *double*-preachers'-kids. Few people can relate to all *that*! But uncommon experiences may still share a common prayer. What I have learned is that so much depends not only on which stories we choose to tell, but on the spirit in which we choose to tell them. "Gently between the words" expresses my hope for intimacy, not of the romantic kind, but of the kind I share with an author like Brian Doyle, whose voice still preaches gently in my head long after I have finished the final page. It is poignant that I write these words on the two-year anniversary of my mentor's death.

Gently Between the Words is dedicated to my middle child, Asa. When he was three-and-a-half years old, our family vacationed at Topsail Beach for spring break. But this was also during Holy Week, so my mind was back in the church office. In fact, I was writing a sermon for Good Friday when Asa ran onto the porch and grabbed my hand. And so I put down my work and off we went together. My son's words still ring in my head. "Daddy, come and walk the whole ocean with me!"

Andrew Taylor-Troutman
Chapel Hill, North Carolina
May 27, 2019

I

MYSTERIES AND EPIPHANIES

I keep writing about the ordinary because for me it's the home of the extraordinary.
—Philip Levine

GRACE DANCE

Waiting, I did what I had done before,
willing the medicine to bring forth calm.
I took my teething boy into my arms
and slowly twirled our creaky wooden floor.
Out in the dark, I heard our lone neighbor
start his truck across rolling fields and farm,
to comfort lambing ewes in his old barn,
riding out what Old Man Winter had in store.

He could not have paid more than a quick glance
to our home, as his headlights bumped and shone.
Twin beams, appearing to us by some chance,
marked his lonely passage through the night.
And yet they stilled my child with their grace dance,
angels flying by in luminous white.

A GRACIOUS PLENTY

For the people of New Dublin Presbyterian Church

knew to find the two old farmers on the far, lonely side of the unused barn. The late fall's setting sun had bitten into the mountain range, while the tractors in the valley were finishing the last of the harvest. As I walked up to these parishioners, their weathered faces broke into smiles beneath their John Deere caps.

Each greeted me with a firm handshake. They no longer worked the fields, but their hands were permanently calloused. I found an old plastic bucket and turned it over, sitting at their feet. They leaned back against the barn and tilted toward each other. Between the two, they'd heard plenty of pastors over the years and seen them come and go. "Short timers," they'd say.

I listened silently to their memories of harvests, bountiful and poor, the farmer's equivalent to the size of a caught fish, until the talk turned to my second son.

"A hearty boy," the shorter of them had said, causing the taller to nod approvingly. I reminded them that our second son was ten pounds at birth and the doctor had told my parents, "Congratulations. He's a toddler!" They chuckled as though they had never heard this well-worn story. A red-tailed hawk screamed in the distance and the three of us silently watched the tractors growing darker in the shadow of the hills.

Finally, the shorter one wondered when my wife and I might try for a third child.

I shook my head, adamantly: "Two's enough."

There was a hint of a smile in the way he looked up at his old friend before turning his attention back to me.

"You sure 'bout that?"

"Yes, sir, I am. We already have a gracious plenty," I added, mimicking what I'd heard them say.

To which the taller replied, "Ain't three a holy number?"

Suddenly, those two grinned like little boys.

———⊷✕⊶———

They both had three children. They were both married for more than fifty years. And both farmed their entire lives except for when they were in the army. Neither talked about the war.

But they both loved to talk about the weather, about the goings-on of the farms, and most of all about their families. One was a Democrat, the other a Republican, and they chided each other, gently. Together, they had been members of our small rural church for one hundred and twenty years and were among the strongest financial supporters. While they were no longer active in leadership, I sought their blessing for every major decision.

They loved to repeat a joke at my expense. One would ask the other if he could recall what I had preached about. "About fifteen minutes," the other would reply. And they would giggle.

Time was fluid behind the barn. The old farmers' memories drifted in and out of the twilight like smoke. Something would remind one of them of a story and in an instant their old friends would be there among us in colorful detail, men with nicknames like Shorty. One time a pigeon suddenly took off from the barn roof and conjured Shorty, way up there in the loft putting up one last square bale of hay, when, without warning—the old farmers recalled—he did a backflip twelve feet down to the floor!

Many of their peers had nicknames, but the title "Mr." was reserved for their mentors. I learned that a successful farmer was made by plenty of hard work, more than a little luck, and the generosity of the community, particularly the older men who gave young farmers a start, a loan, or forgave a debt. Both farmers would tear up at the mention of these quietly gracious men and their quirks: He always knocked his boots off away from the house when he came to visit; he smoked with his pipe clamped between his teeth; he prayed in a high-pitched, nasal voice.

"I've been blessed with good friends," one of them would say.

"A gracious plenty," the other would respond.

Both were so generous to me.

———— ⌘ ————

That Advent was the year my one-year-old son contracted walking pneumonia. Then, my wife caught mono. My older boy and I succumbed to double sinus infections. All of us were miserable for weeks. Just when my wife and I would be at our wits' end, the doorbell would ring and a casserole would be left on the back step, a friendly hand waving from the driver's seat as the truck backed down our gravel driveway.

A few days before Christmas, my family woke to the surprising sight of a giant pile of horse manure out in our garden, a weathered shovel tied with a red ribbon sticking out of "the big *poop*," as our oldest delighted in saying. "Black gold" was what those two farmers called it. They had another saying, that pastors were like manure: Spread us out and we can do some good, but get a pile of us together and we stink to high heaven!

By Christmas Eve, I was well enough to preach or, at least, show up. For as long as anybody could remember, the Christmas Eve service began at 8 p.m. Not ideal for young children, but the farming families all attended with their grandchildren and great-grandchildren home for the holiday. In previous years, the two old farmers would be the first ones to lift their burning candles during the last carol, "Silent Night," signaling to the rest of us to do the same.

But this year, the shorter one was plagued all evening by coughing spells. After the service was over and candles had been blown out, a nurse in the congregation pressed him to go to the hospital. I knew he would refuse. His family was home, the youngest daughter all the way from New York City with her two daughters, her youngest named after his wife. He was sitting in the pew, protesting that he was just fine, and I knelt down to offer a prayer. This is what you do. You show up. And you speak common words like "bless" and "heal" and "God." You say "Amen" and you hope in the Infinite Incomprehensibility. That's what the old farmer used to call the Lord Almighty.

But, for once, he didn't even speak. His face glistened with tears.

———∞∞∞———

This was also the time when Brian Doyle, one of my writing mentors, shared publicly that he had "a big honkin' brain tumor." It was like him to make light of his situation, but he understood the seriousness of his diagnosis. It turned out that this would be Brian's last Christmas as well.

Years ago, I first wrote to Mr. Doyle because I'd treasured his first-person narratives in magazines as diverse as *Christian Century* and *The Sun.* For all the charms of pastoring a rural congregation and raising young children, your world becomes pretty small. I inhaled Brian's stories from different places and times, and I wanted him to know how much his stories meant to me.

He was gracious with his response, and every other month or so we'd mail short essays and poems across the country to each other. Born in New York, having worked in Chicago, and then living in Oregon, Brian had never been to this part of the Appalachian Mountains and was curious about the topography as well as the people, for he said that all beings are holy (except the New York Yankees baseball team).

I sent him little notes about the old farmers. How they said about parenting that life was best between diapers and dating. How they said about snow that it was a poor man's fertilizer. How they did not like Wendell Berry, another of my favorite writers, because Mr. Berry was critical of tractors.

Both of them had started farming with mules, and they remembered one of those stubborn creatures biting and kicking an innocent boy, and it would be a cold day in hell before they ever wrote poems about *them*! Brian chortled over that line.

I sent Brian a nostalgic paragraph about one lazy afternoon, before my wife and I had children, when I had stood in the gravel driveway, watching the late summer light ooze in the air like honey, listening to this old farmer (the shorter one) tell me that, when I did have kids, the school bus would come all the way down the gravel road to drop them off right in front of my house.

In response, Brian sent me a poem called "Lily" about a father who "shambles" to his car one morning at the same moment a school bus "bounces" past him. These delightfully contrasting verbs set the scene: "a little cheerful kid waves to me." Brian's daughter is named Lily, which is apparent enough to any reader. But what happens next in the poem calls for interpretation. Reflecting on that little cheerful kid, the speaker of the poem realizes that "for a moment I am / That kid and she is my daughter and I'm waving to her / Hoping she will wave to me."

It is a mystery, these extraordinary epiphanies in the ordinariness of life, like what Brian described in his poem or like praying for that old farmer on Christmas Eve. I only know that, in such moments as these, I realize that eternity breaks into time and all of us are actually a part of everything and everyone else. Even the Yankees.

———⌇———

A few months after Christmas, I knew to find the taller one in his living room. After his friend's death, he no longer returned to lean against that old barn. I didn't blame him.

But, that day, I had good news. The *best* news, in fact. I wasn't telling everybody in the congregation. Not yet. But my wife was …

"Pregnant," he finished for me. "You don't say!" He started laughing, and I joined him. Then, suddenly, we were both crying, for we were grieving, too. Through his window, we watched the tractors plowing the fields in the distance. It is a grace in ministry, as in life, when you know people deeply enough to let the silence speak.

Finally, wiping his eyes, the old farmer said, "You think he had anything to do with it? You know …"

"Us having a third child?"

He nodded, very slowly.

I shrugged. I told him I sure didn't know the Infinite Incomprehensibility. But I liked his idea. We smiled together.

"I'll bet she'll have a little girl, just like he would have wanted."

A little more than six months later, our daughter was born. Weighing a little more than eight pounds, she was not as big as her brothers, but still a gracious plenty.

SIGNS AND WONDERS

Except ye see signs and wonders, ye will not believe.
—John 4:48

It was our first visit. I sat on the sofa in her living room surrounded by pictures of their four children, eight grandchildren. The shades were drawn against the sunlight as we chatted: get-to-know-you preliminaries about where I was from, the obligatory lament concerning the weather (I forget, now, whether it had rained too much or too little). Her recently deceased husband was all around us in picture frames.

There he was in their most recent church directory photo, smiling above her right shoulder, his moustache trimmed, his tie cleanly knotted. From another frame, he watched us somber-faced, dressed in his police uniform, his eyes kind. There he was at Christmas, kneeling before the artificial tree, his grin merry and bright, and at the Thanksgiving table, carving tools paused above the turkey. The oldest picture was a shot of him standing waist deep in the pool, bare-chested, sunglassed, a suntanned daughter giggling in his hairy arms.

She watched me as I took them all in: "He still comes to me at night."

Her blue eyes intent, judging my reaction.

"I wake every night about three. There's a small dot of light in the far corner of our bedroom. It's no bigger than a firefly at first. But as soon as I see it, it grows to the size of a flashlight. Then goes up the wall, across the ceiling, until coming to a stop right above my head. The light waits there on the ceiling until I close my eyes. When I open them, he's gone. Until the next night, that is."

I was a young pastor, still wet behind the ears from seminary, and this was my first inkling that most of what I thought I knew for certain, I actually didn't.

⁂

A parishioner once told me that ever since his father died, he'd been visited by a large black butterfly. Its wings were like wet coal, glimmering slick. He works outside on his dad's rental properties. The black butterfly only arrives when he is working hard at what he is supposed to do.

⁂

Another man's wife died, and yellow flowers poked up from the mulch by the mailbox. Like a special delivery, these flowers appeared overnight about a week after she was in the ground. In the backyard, she'd planted flowers for fifty years, but he'd never seen anything quite like these. Their petals tended toward a tulip, yet were smaller. A new neighbor told him the name: crocus. Crocuses are usually purple, but he learned you could find yellow ones.

"Looked it up on the Internet," he said, "and discovered this Greek legend about two young lovers granted immortality. There was also a Christian tale about Saint Valentine who'd sent a crocus to a jailer's blind daughter. She smelled that flower and got her sight back. Do you believe it?"

He did not give me the chance to respond.

"Anyways, Pastor, what I really wanted to tell you was how I saw sunshine yellow crocuses around her tombstone this very week."

She stayed by her husband's side throughout his long and difficult illness. From his bed, he would greet her whenever she walked back into the room: "I haven't taken the last train to Chicago."

As the funeral home workers pushed the gurney bearing his corpse out of their home, a cell phone rang. The ringtone was a locomotive's whistle! The young employee saw the widow burst into tears, and he began to apologize, thinking he had been disrespectful. She just shook her head. How could she explain?

———ꙮ———

Another widow had been trying for years to coax bluebirds into nesting along their fence. She had the birdhouses, of course, but had also researched the types of food that attracted them. She'd cooked this oatmeal-like substance with mealworms in it, which had cost more than their own supper. Nothing worked. That winter, she'd spent so much time beside her husband's hospital bed that she couldn't even keep the feeders full of seed for the usual customers.

You can guess who arrived about two weeks after he passed. She'd finished the dishes, like always, then stepped out onto the porch, into the deepening chill. The bluebirds zipped to the tree he'd named after their youngest daughter, Carol. And this widow listened to the bluebirds sing, caroling just for her.

———ꙮ———

He comes to his daughter whenever she is under anesthesia. He died of colon cancer, so she is vigilant about her screenings. Every three years, he comes to her. This last time he drove a shiny black Cadillac. So unlike him! He honked the horn, then reached over with his long arm to push open the passenger door. She'd sat, buckled up, asked where they were going. He said he had no idea. So unlike him!

"But he still had the same twinkle in his eyes," she said, a mixture of grief and wonder in her voice, before telling me how he had driven her along winding roads until she awoke in the white recovery room.

———⊗⊗⊗———

I officiated a graveside service on top of a hill at a family farm. I'd just pronounced the benediction when tendrils of dried hay positively leaped into the air, spiraling like they were draining up into the blue sky.

"It's a sign," one person cried. "It's like angel wings," commented another. "No, it has to do with changing currents producing a vortex," explained a gentleman. "I see it all the time," he added.

Then, there was silence as we watched the hay in the air against the backdrop of the green hills.

———⊗⊗⊗———

At funerals, I'm probably as guilty as any preacher of talking in dualities: light verses dark, body verses spirit, life verses afterlife. From the pulpit on Sunday, there are times when I want to draw a bright line separating the difference between either right or wrong, either good or evil.

But a faith *lived* is often a paradox, both the creative and precarious tension of holding two together: both hope and doubt, both comfort and challenge, both "Amen" and "O Lord, why?" The kingdom of heaven is both here and not yet. The mystery is never explained and often brings tears to our eyes.

When that widow told me about her husband returning to her every night as a light in the dark, I eagerly offered rational explanations: It was probably passing traffic, a trick of the light, the reflection of something outside.

Her eyes sharp and bright, that wise woman leaned forward in her chair and looked at me, hard.

"Don't try and explain it to me."

THE VERBS OF THEM

I love how the farmer's son,
when called for the children's sermon,
slip-slides from a hard-backed pew,
cowboy boots slamming
one, two
on the cracked wooden floor.

I love to watch
as this boy suddenly flops
into the aisle, giggling,
ready for Daddy to scoop up
his loose-limbed human spaghetti
and tickle with calloused, tender hands.

I love the verbs of them
as they are now walking,
both grinning ear to ear,
both stepping in time
one, two.

In the twinkling of an eye,
such moments fly away forever.
That's why I love the verbs of them.

DAFFODILS

For the people of Raleigh Moravian Church

My earliest memory of Dad's church is autographing the Order of Service. A pastor's kid knows not to call the paper the usher hands out a "program." Because worship is not the circus. (One hopes, anyway.) With a pencil taken from the hymnal rack behind the pew, I would scrawl my name over and over again, practicing for when I was famous. After all, everyone in the sanctuary knew my name.

Ms. Joyce knew every child in Sunday school. She told us that God delighted in making the daffodils for us. But, since they were growing outside our classroom, we should leave them in the ground so that adults could enjoy them, too. We took this seriously because Ms. Joyce took us seriously.

When she taught the lesson, she would sit on the floor and look at us through her round, owl-eyed glasses. She wore her hair pulled back into a rather severe bun, but she smiled easily. "Jesus" was always a good answer to any Sunday school query, but if you raised your hand and asked a question in return, Ms. Joyce would brightly respond, "Good thought!" This would cause you to sit up a little straighter, even if you didn't know Noah from, say, Adam.

I'll never forget all those annual church yard sales when it always rained yet never dampened the spirits of the faithful, who lugged their basement junk from their cars to the folding tables—the loaves and fishes that fed the five thousand, the handheld radios and flower pots that balanced our church budget. And Ms. Joyce would give each child a new-to-you toy like a Superman figurine or the green plastic army gun that Mom would make you give back.

Remember how strange and vaguely upsetting it was to see your kindergarten or first-grade teacher out in public? We thought that person could only exist in front of the familiar chalkboard and never in the grocery aisle. As with our cereal, we like our people in predictable boxes.

But in addition to being our Sunday school teacher, Ms. Joyce also ran a plumbing company with her husband. After she died, the parking lot at my father's church was filled with trucks, pick-ups that had pipes and plungers standing at attention in the beds. The joke was that the city had better shut off the main water valve, for no matter the plumbing emergency, none of the workers were leaving Ms. Joyce's funeral.

I came to find out that those dozens of burly, heavily tattooed men with Old Testament beards who filled up a third of the packed sanctuary all called her "Mama." I spoke with one of them in the fellowship hall after Dad's benediction. His beefy hand was loading up a dainty china plate with a leaning tower of crackers and cheese.

"Yeah, I sure gone miss Mama," he lamented. "She made you feel special, you know?"

Yeah, I did.

Walking to my car, I carried my Order of Service with its printed liturgy. And I had the good thought that the daffodils were praying, too.

IN TIME TO COME

*For everything there is a season, and a time for
every matter under heaven.*

—Ecclesiastes 3:1

You, dear godfather, were my first babysitter
and now, at eighty-five years old, you know
more about a MacBook than I do. I enjoyed
your recent e-mail with the description of how
the Genius "emerged from the hinterland" of the
Apple store. I think you can use "hinterland" with
authority since you have farmed your whole life in
the Canadian Rockies.

Instead of your farm, you now write from a
small townhome in an assisted living community. It
is hard for me to picture you there, but I know your
lovely wife is with you. And I join you in prayers
of gratitude for your successful knee replacement
operation. I'm especially grateful that you have
resumed your early morning walks through the
cemetery where your mother is buried. You noted
in a recent e-mail, "Charles Dickens was also fond
of walking before first light."

Thank you for your birthday gift. I am already halfway through *The Shepherd's Life* by James Rebanks and duly noted the one passage you had underlined: "Like all good grandparents my grandfather could only see the best in me, and that always made me stand a little taller."

I love how you wrote "godfather, too!" in the margin.

Just the other day, I met with a young couple at church about the sacrament of baptism for their infant. In the course of our discussion, I told them about our story, how my parents originally met in Winston-Salem, North Carolina, but that I was born in your little farming community outside of Edmonton, Alberta, because Dad had agreed to serve your rural church as a seminary intern. I told those young parents that, alongside family members and other caregivers, godparents witness the baptism of infants and make vows to teach and nurture the child as she or he matures in stature and faith. This young father joked that he had known about a "godfather" only from the mobster movie!

I'm glad you received my note with Wendell Berry's line: "Planting trees early in spring, / we make a place for birds to sing / in time to come." I think of you as an optimist, as well as a planter of trees. In a sermon a few weeks ago, I mentioned the hopeful story of how you had formed a bond with your Muslim friend from Iran by planting hundreds of trees, singing in two-part harmony that folk rendition of the famous passage in Ecclesiastes. "There is a season ... turn, turn, turn."

As the song goes, there is a time to plant and a time to reap, a time to laugh and a time to weep. Your farm is now a Wal-Mart. I remember how you wrote of the bulldozers ravaging your nineteenth-century barns and buildings. As you wisely say, "I frequently remind myself that this journey is a long series of adjustments."

Recently, I have noticed that you have included a different refrain in your e-mails. You write that you are feeling well enough but are quick to add, "I'm on the front lines now." You wrote of the death of your friend and fellow planter of trees: "He was prepared to go on ahead and so am I. I have the feeling that he will be there to welcome me."

I wonder if this thought comes to you while strolling by the tombstones in the quiet darkness.

In your new home, you report that there is still room for a Christmas tree, including "the lovely hand-stitched jar ring decorations" my mom made for you the year I was born. With a Mason jar lid, a piece of burlap, and a little thread, she made a Christmas star that has stood the test of time, connecting us across borders. As we sing, blest be the ties that bind.

I have always appreciated the yarns you have spun, particularly the story of how you came to live on that old farm so many years ago. Around 3:30 p.m. in early February 1971, you drove away from your father-in-law's fields after helping him haul hay. Instead of turning left at the end of the lane like usual and going to your new bride in your rented home, you turned right. You had "a nudge or something" to check on an older couple from church who had been absent for a couple of Sundays. Ms. Violet had just taken cinnamon buns out of the oven. Soon there was piping hot tea to go with them. Mr. George confessed he had lung problems and, before the tea had cooled, shared with you that they were thinking of selling their place. You lived there for the next forty-three years.

There at your new Mac, many miles away, you marvel anew at retelling this story: "How do things like that happen? An angel must've been sitting on my shoulder and prompted me to turn right. *Right?*"

Maybe an angel with a guitar singing, "Turn, turn, turn."

II

CONTRADICTIONS
AND MULTITUDES

*The truth will set you free. But not until it is
finished with you.*
—David Foster Wallace

SUNDAYS FROM NOW

Sundays from now
I'll tell of a white flowing gown
sewn by Gran's hand,
and how your tiny fierce grip
clutched timeless vows.

Sundays from now
I'll tell of plain old tap water
warm to the touch,
and how "into His death" speaks
of Divine love.

Sundays from now
I'll tell of the shimmering drops
across your skin,
and how the church grinned as one
when you looked out.

Sundays from now
I'll pray that your shining eyes still
brim with surprise,
at how a shimmer of Vast
sprinkles this Now.

SPILLS

You woman ... taught me to love loving
with my eyes wide open ...
—Jaki Shelton Green

The day she died I wrote a spill for my Gran. It went something like this ...

Gran made giant pots of spaghetti that would have fed armies, and hordes of buttered, crescent yeast rolls.

Gran snapped string beans on her back porch as her mother and her grandmother had done in the same North Carolina summers.

When I was maybe seven years old, I marched over to Gran and reported that I was going to push over one of the giant oaks in her yard. She smiled at me. "Go ahead," she invited me to try.

As a boy, I would stretch up on my toes so she could kiss my cheek. In college, I would lean down so she could peck that exact same spot.

Gran never smiled in pictures because she hated her crooked teeth.

How long has it been since Gran knew who I was? Three years? Four years?

Gran was always looking out of the house for us when my family's minivan pulled up her driveway—her face in the kitchen window like a full moon.

This kind of "spill" is of course a writing exercise. It's something anyone can do. You just write whatever comes to mind without pausing or editing. Let the words pour out onto the page and see what seemingly disparate thoughts run together, pooling like a reflective puddle.

When my first son was born in the fall of 2012, we took him to meet his Great Gran the week before Christmas. My uncle drove her from the assisted living community to my aunt's church where we sat in the parlor. Gran seemed agitated by these unfamiliar surroundings. She could still recognize family members with a gentle prompting: "I'm Andrew. *Andrew*. Anna's son. Your first *grandson*." She kissed my cheek. "And this ... this is your first *great*-grandson."

Gran eased the baby down on his back onto her knees, careful to support his head. My boy squirmed. "Whoa now," she smiled, "careful not to spill you."

———∞∞∞———

That old saying about "no use crying over spilt milk" has been around since 1738, according to the Online Etymology Dictionary. But here in 2019, I sure feel like crying when my younger son spills his milk. Now his shirt needs to be changed. And his baby sister is sobbing because her diaper is wet. All the while the oldest boy gleefully showers Cheerios across the floor like confetti. My cell phone is blowing up—a modern idiom of violence and disaster. The kids had me up in the night, and now my head thuds in time with the spilt milk dripping onto the floor. I see that we are out of paper towels. I am frustrated as hell, but there's no use in crying. I sop up the spill with toilet paper.

———∞∞∞———

Three years after Gran met our firstborn, we brought the second baby boy to visit her. Down the hall from her tiny room in the memory care unit, there was a library with shelves filled with new Bibles and worn Danielle Steele paperbacks. The slanting morning light made the dust sparkle in the air. My older son named the wild animals pictured in old copies of *Field and Stream* lying on a wooden coffee table. Gran warily regarded him as something like a wild animal. She briefly turned her attention to the baby dozing in his car seat on the floor. Then, she turned her wheelchair away. This was Christmas 2015. Her mind was slipping, she was just trying to hold on, and I cried later in the parking lot because something precious had been lost. What is spilled can never be put back.

We never tried to introduce Gran to her first great-granddaughter.

The online dictionary reveals to me a complex history of the word "spill."

One meaning derived from the Danish *spilde* is to lose or waste. When Gran's memory began to fade, it felt like we were losing her slowly, as if she were still with us and yet not with us at the same time. With those persistent and unstoppable spills of her memory, what complex and rich history, what vital and caring personality, was our family losing?

Continuing to peruse the dictionary, I learn that in 1845, if you had a spill, it meant you were thrown from a horse. And in nautical terms, it means to let the wind out of a sail.

Losing Gran has thrown me. Her death has let the wind out of my sails.

———— ∞ ————

Gran used to whisper-sing old Baptist hymns at her sewing machine, which was why I thought that machine was called a Singer.

Gran fried us hamburgers for breakfast and let us eat dinner on TV trays while watching baseball or *The Andy Griffith Show.* She taught me to whistle that opening tune.

Gran had such a high tolerance for pain that she had root canals without any numbing.

Gran didn't object when my brother got his ears pierced with silver hoops. Instead she said he should have come to her. She'd have done it for free with a needle and an ice cube—just like she did with her own daughters.

A child of the Depression, Gran saved buttons in a jar so that each one might be reused. And she taught herself how to fix the leaky faucet and unclog the toilet in order to save money on a plumber.

Gran grew up with Jim Crow and didn't think it was safe to swim in the same pool with black people.

Gran used to tell me that "the blacks were happier when they were slaves."

———⊶⊷———

I learn from the dictionary that the definition of "spill" that I most often use—the one we think of when a toddler knocks over his milk, "to let (liquid) fall or run out"—developed in the mid-fourteenth century in reference to the spilling of blood. Going even further back in time, the Old English derivation from *spillan* meant to destroy, mutilate, or kill.

To spill, then, is an act rooted in violence and bloodshed.

It is impossible to spill about my Gran without spilling some uncomfortable truths about her and her thinking. Those spills reflect back to me my uncomfortable legacy as a white man raised in the South.

———⊶⊷———

My church recently hosted Sonny Kelly, a local storyteller, scholar, and activist, in his one-man performance of *The Talk*. Not a show about "the birds and the bees," this talk was about the painful conversations black parents must have with their children about racism in America. He shared that his play was inspired by a conversation he had with his young son and how he wrestled with what to say. How could he prepare his child to survive in a world that routinely and systematically enacts violence against black men, women, and children? How can he reassure his child that he is safe, when he knows that because of the color of his skin, he is not?

10 and 2. You always keep your hands on 10 and 2. If you're white like me, it's to keep you safe while the car is moving. If you're black like Sonny Kelly, it's to keep you safe when your car is stopped. By the police. By the protectors of our community.

Listening to *The Talk*, I recalled a time when I was a child and my little brother accidentally dialed 9-1-1. A police officer came to our home, and my brother solemnly promised to never do it again. Then the nice policeman walked away, taking his gleaming gun with him.

I think white parents want to shield our kids from the difficult realities of race in order to protect our family histories. Don't spill your secrets. But if Sonny Kelly must have a talk with his children about racism, my talk with my children must be about anti-racism. About the grave inheritance of our white advantage and the responsibility we bear to write a different story, a different and better reality.

Yes, you can clean up the spilt milk. Even with toilet paper. But we cannot clean up the spilt blood. We must stop trying to whitewash our American history. It only repeats itself when we do. We must come to terms with the reality that our past was violent and our present is too. Racism hurts us all. It dehumanizes us all.

———⋙⋘———

Someday I will spill to my children the secrets of our family and of our past. In my shared memories of Gran, I will tell them how she mistrusted people just because of their skin color. How she lived in a world that made black people use separate water fountains and learn in separate schools. How she was a part of that world and, as far as I know, didn't question it. But I will also tell them how she cared for her family. How she sewed beautiful baptismal gowns and made the best sizzling hot fried chicken.

Your Great Gran, she loved peaches, just like you. And you, my child, have inherited the peachy hue of her skin and all the advantages afforded by our society to those who are deemed white. Like you, like me, your Great Gran was beautiful and tragic, fearful and brave, ignorant and wise, living and breathing and flawed and beloved by God. Do you understand?

"Daddy? When can we watch TV?"

———⋙⋘———

On MLK day, I took my sons to the local library. As they sat there coloring—the oldest one so very careful to crayon inside the lines, the younger scrawling with abandon—another child about five years old skipped over. Her skin was the color of honeyed cinnamon, her dark hair braided into a dozen strands with glittering pink balls tied to each one. Now three heads were bent over the same page, their red, blond, and black hair nearly touching as they colored in purple, pink, and orange. Like a sunrise. Like, I prayed, the dawning of a new day.

David Foster Wallace once wrote that the truth will set you free. But not until it is finished with you.

On the Sunday Gran died, I baptized a little girl sixteen months old. As the drops of water from the font spilled down this child's rosy cheeks, tears came to my eyes, tears witnessing to unending grace that knows neither limit of time nor space. As the water spilled, I remembered how Gran held my firstborn, how Gran held me when I was a child, and how I held Gran's hand for the last time, just a few days before.

The truth will set us free.

My faith community stands at the baptism font. We invite our children. We cup our hands and lift the water and, if the light is right, catch a vision of our reflections, a vision of our skins, and we glimpse all our contradictions and multitudes, our worry lines, and the crinkles around our eyes from all the pain and laughter. We remember how Jesus put his skin into the game because he loves the little children, all the children of the world.

The truth will set us free. But not until it is finished with us.

As I stare into this reflective pool, I know that baptism is a distinctive Christian sacrament, which has been used to divide, even to conquer. But I remember a freeing truth: No religion or creed has an exclusive claim to water. Every drop of rain eventually spills back into the sea. And I remember how each of us emerges from the waters of a mother. How each of us is made of water and requires water to live. How a child at sixteen months might splash and play in a little water. How all children are finally *our* children.

I hope truth will set us free.

BEHOLDEN

Behold! I make all things new.
—Revelation 21:5

You, child, just crushed your paper cup,
and discarded it near my feet.
A gulp of lemonade's a mere

moment's reprieve from your dancing
with fireflies, never quite
catching lightning in your hands.

Now you roll down the grassy hill,
drop all the way to the bottom
and look up. You take a bow, love.

If you were within gentle reach,
could I make time stand still,
and peer through the cracks

of my own cupped fingers and
broken past, gazing down as
your light illuminates my dark?

I marvel at your glow,
your contradictions and multitudes,
the newness and wholeness of you.

You continue to bow deeply
and I keep watch from a distance,
my wine in clear plastic tumbler

now forgotten, as I imbibe
flickers of lost light. Grass-stained knees,
come to me please! That I may

cup your chin, my palm leaking time,
which rolls to where, I pray,
we can both be whole again and new.

INSIDE OUT BOYS

Go outside. Look up. Secret of life.
—Anne Lamott

Ginny and I are raising our children only about thirty miles from where I grew up. As I write from my desk overlooking our street, there's an epic game of hide-and-seek taking place outside a neighbor's townhome. I catch glimpses of my two boys, darting and dashing, laughing with abandon.

My younger brother was my childhood best friend. He and I would scarf breakfast, then I would race him down the steps, two-by-two, and into the green grass to throw the football. We'd play basketball at our elementary school across the street. We'd grab our bikes so that I could teach him to ride with no hands, balancing with arms stretched to the sides like an airplane.

"Me and you," my brother would say, "we're outside boys."

Our father was the pastor and we were always inside church on Sunday mornings. The sanctuary had a brick floor and only one window high on the far wall, which I never paid much attention to as a young boy seated next to Mom in the front. Years later, as a high schooler in the back left pew—the Amen Corner, my preacher father christened it—I would stare out that window, envying the branches waving free in the wind while I sat trapped in a never-ending service, usually still hungover from the night before.

Now, at my writing desk, I watch my boys playing innocently outside, and more memories of my youth dart in and dash out.

I remember that some high school dudes could sport a five o'clock shadow and pass for twenty-one, at least at certain seedy establishments downtown. But my friends and I got our beer by asking homeless men to buy it for us. It was a strategy-turned-game we called "Hey Mister."

I'd find myself tromping through dark alleys that reeked of urine, nervously passing a twenty-dollar bill to a man who, I assumed, had recently pissed on the grungy graffiti scrawled across the dumpsters. We would tell him he could "keep the change," trying to make the illegal activity enticing. More than a few "Misters" took off with all of our money, which meant that I would curse heavily in order to mask my sense of relief. If we got the case of beer, my friends and I would chug as fast as we could, grimacing against the taste, and stumble off to find something to do.

Perhaps there would be a party at some kid's house where the parents were out of town. The music would summon us inside. On the periphery of the dancing, I might glimpse another boy steering a girl toward a couch in the shadows. My friends and I would often leave on foot. We would sprint through neighborhoods on numbed legs, shoes pounding the pavement, lungs burning.

When I left home for college, I wouldn't have to venture far for my beer; I could just stay inside the fraternity house.

Years later, in seminary, I would read about Teresa of Avila's "interior castle." She envisioned the soul's search for union with God—through prayer and meditation—as a kind of journey into a diamond castle, where the soul moves from the outer darkness through the castle's seven chambers, each leading more deeply to its center, where God dwells in each of us. Through the mystery of prayer, we journey from darkness into a divine inner light.

But, when it came to those fraternity parties, the deeper inside you went, the more darkness you found. I risked not returning from the depths of alcohol and drugs.

———— ∞ ————

I had forgotten about this guy from my high school until old photos started showing up on my Facebook feed. He came back to me as a huge presence, literally, at over six feet tall and two hundred pounds, and metaphorically, because he was always the life of the party, the personality that filled up a room. His obituary began by listing how he had loved hunting and fishing, anything to do with being outdoors. The obituary ended with a plea for support for those on the inside of our heroin epidemic.

A few more clicks on my screen revealed his public record. He was adding felonies for larceny to his criminal record around the time Ginny and I were adding children to our family. He and I hailed from the same hometown; we were at the same parties. He was an outside boy, too, but he became trapped inside his addiction. I wonder if someone could have made a difference.

I remember a walk with my campus pastor.

My college's campus pastor was a short man with a bald head and a bushy beard just above his clerical collar. When he spoke, he gestured with great excitement, his hands like two birds attempting to land in the nest of his beard.

He led the chapel service every Wednesday morning, but, more often, I ran into him late

Saturday nights when I was with friends, walking back to the dorms from the fraternity houses. His energetic little black dog, Pepper, seemed to tug him along until he fell into step with us. We stumbled and cursed. Someone would stop to pee in the bushes. Occasionally, someone would want to talk theology, perhaps slurring the Good Lord's name. But Pastor never uttered the slightest hint of judgment. If the drunken dialogue dried up, he would tell stories about Pepper's heroic yet futile attempts as a hunter of squirrels and, before we knew it, we would be safely back at the dorm. Pastor would call out a blessing as the doors closed behind us. If you lingered in the darkened lobby, you would see his retreating figure in the moonlight going back to make sure of someone else.

Once, I called out to him. And he came back. As we continued our walk, he hardly said a word. But as I poured out my confession about my drinking and drugging, something fell into step with us. As we walked beneath the starry sky, I sensed the gentle footsteps of something like hope.

Why do teenagers turn to drugs and alcohol? A search engine could give you a list of reasons.

As a preacher's son, my rebellion against religion was explicitly tied to challenging my father. Now that I am also a pastor, he and I talk shop.

Now that I am clean and sober, we do analyze those adolescent days. My recipe for (almost) disaster started with a heaping, steaming, double-dose of anxiety about how I looked on the outside and how I felt deep down inside. Add a dash of curiosity, a dollop of boredom, and bake at sixteen years old with hormones raging.

It's important to my ongoing recovery that I take responsibility for my actions. But my father believes that he, and to a certain extent the larger Christian culture, turned a blind eye to our parties, unwilling to face the truth. He and I discuss Robert Bly's book *Iron John*, which uses an ancient fairy tale to make the case that modern boys will become men through the guidance of elder men in their community. Bly contends it is the sacred duty of elders to bless young men. While I find gender roles in Bly's work too restrictive, my life bears witness to the importance of men as mentors. *Men*-tors.

Before my college pastor, Granddad embodied this guiding presence. He did not go to church, but Granddad could put the fear of God in me. In contrast to a church that turns a blind eye, Grandad's look was piercing. No one in our family ever wanted to be caught in the crosshairs of his disapproving stare.

As a boy, I learned the hard way that Granddad did not abide foul language. I dropped one—and only one—four-letter word during a game of pool in his basement. Granddad reached across the table to put down his cue stick right in front of where I stood. Mom reports that he used to hand her a dictionary to look up ten words that she could have used instead. But that one look was enough for me.

He smoked a pipe after supper. Even now, I can hear the whisper of a struck match and catch the faint smell of sweet smoke. He and I would share cookie salads—two Oreos and a Chips Ahoy. I never knew him to drink anything but milk or water. Dad says his father-in-law enjoyed the occasional scotch, but the brain tumor took Granddad before I'd had my first drink.

The desk where I write is of smooth wood the color of a worn penny, its dark grains visible beneath a few scratches made by my sons' errant pen strokes. They both like to sneak in here and doodle on my sermon notes.

Besides a few loose-leaf pages, there's enough table space for my laptop, an open book, a framed selfie of my wife and me against a backdrop of snowy pine trees, an old wooden bowl that was part of Granddad's shaving kit, and a picture of him and me.

There's three-year-old me sitting in Granddad's lap. He wears a homemade, tri-corner hat that was folded from shiny red paper. He relaxes in a collared shirt with the top button undone, his dark blue tie loosened. My right hand has a fistful of that tie, as if to pull his attention toward me, and I brandish a plastic white spoon in my other hand. The left corner of his mouth is slightly upturned. There's an unmistakable brightness in his eyes behind his thick-framed glasses. And I can still hear what he always said: "Whoa now."

Granddad was spending the night at our house when he had The Nightmare. At the breakfast table the next morning, he reported that he had dreamed he was being chased by an enormous, angry bear that he could not escape. A few weeks later, his doctors found the brain tumor. He would be dead in six months. I was just a few months from starting high school.

Granddad refused to allow my younger brother or me to see him as he lay dying. "I will not let them see me like *this*," he told my mom.

After years of ministry, I have witnessed what Granddad called *this*: the chapped lips touched by the wet pink sponge, the changing of bed sheets by efficient hands and a clucking tongue, the labored breathing known as a death rattle, and the eyes of the one in the bed, which hold the pain until finally glazing over, staring blankly at some corner of the ceiling. *This* may be teary, boring, smelly, and long. *This* can also be a daughter's hands over her ears as her father once again screams, "I can't keep the damn door shut!"

But *this* can be beautiful: a granddaughter falling asleep on her granddad's shoulder, holding his hand as he breathes and then does not. I wonder how differently my adolescence might have been if I had been given even a small glimpse of Granddad's *this*.

Time is only frozen in pictures. To live is to suffer loss, to love is to ache. I have come to believe that you must look the snarling bear in the face.

As I look at the picture of us on my desk, more memories of Granddad come back to me, filling the air like pipe smoke ...

Granddad stands in front of his bathroom mirror with his razor, each stroke mowing cleanly through the shaving cream on his strong jaw. I slip my feet into his enormous bedroom slippers, crossing and uncrossing my toes, my eyes darting from his reflection in the mirror to the bright morning visible through the bedroom window. Over the sound of my brother watching cartoons in the living room, I hear our baseball gloves screaming for us to hustle out into the yard. We are always the Atlanta Braves because that is Granddad's team. He had followed them from his boyhood when they played in Boston, his hometown. Still shaving, Granddad wears his idea of a smile as he diligently works the foamy lather in his wooden bowl with a horsehair brush. Finally, finally, he pats his face dry with a towel and issues the words I long to hear:

"Ready to go outside?"

Even after hours of playing catch, my brother and I have to hustle to match Granddad's long stride, as he circles the perimeter of his lawn, tossing fallen sticks back into the woods. Having endured this chore, I pull him by the hand beneath the trees, and we hike to the bottom of the hill where his property ends at a creek. We pretend to fish, poking leaves drifting in the water with sticks. My brother sits on the bank. Granddad's arm is wrapped around my waist so that I can get close to the edge and lean over the water. I never want to go back inside.

My sons love their granddad. They call my father "Papi." He indulges them with sugar and even sweeter attention. He takes them to parks and playgrounds and, most recently, on a city bus touring the sky-scraping towers. And as they lurched forward, the youngest asked, "Will you keep me *safe*?"

Recently, I prayed with a father whose boy had started smoking marijuana. His son is in the fifth grade. My wife and I try to protect our children. We hope to maintain their innocence a little while longer, prolonging the days of chalk, those smiley faces and rainbows on the sidewalk, and airy afternoons of hide-and-seek when everyone who is lost is always found. But we can't always keep them safe. We pray for help, help from people in our families and faith communities, people of character—as my father says—whose insides match their outsides. That's a good line from Dad. One day, he might give a grandson a hard look at the right time.

———— ∞ ————

I am a pastor now, and I know parents who have lost children. We worship in a sanctuary called Chapel in the Pines. Large windows afford views of surrounding evergreens—"a timbered choir," Wendell Berry would say. Squint and you might see a glint of heaven's light in the treetops. Directly overhead are wooden beams emanating like sun rays from the center. Visible wooden pegs hold these rafters in place. But what you cannot see are the slips of paper, folded into the holes before the pegs were inserted. These are the handwritten prayers of charter members, people whose visions and hopes are always above our heads, prayers without ceasing.

As I sit with grieving parents, I am often silent, for I don't pretend to know either the reasons why or the depths of their hell. But I sense that others are speaking to us. Praying over us. And not just in the sanctuary either. That's why, the older I get and the less I know what to say, the more I suggest to those parents that we go for a walk outside.

———∞∞∞———

As I sit at my desk, deep in thought, I see from my window that the game of hide-and-seek has finally ended and my boys are heading home. In a moment, they'll climb the steps of our front porch and burst inside like bottle rockets. Turning from my desk, I will give them my full attention when they joyfully explode into my bedroom. My two lightnings in a bottle. I will hold them for as long as they will let me.

But, first, I pick up Granddad's shaving bowl from my desk. Across the road, there is a slender pine leaning in the wind. As exacting and precise as he was with his razor, I wish to write about how this tree suddenly calls Granddad to mind—the way he, too, was tall and skinny, yet sturdy and agile. How I can see the wiggle in the corner of his mouth as he sets his briefcase down in the carport. I am running ahead of my brother, and Granddad frees his hand just as I crash into his leg in the hugging style of little boys. His hand is as gentle as a breeze on the back of my neck. And he says what he always says: "Whoa now."

THE PARDON

*You can change a person's life
by saying just one thing, just once.*
—Charlotte Matthews

I started high school in 1995. That spring, my baseball coach announced to the entire P.E. class that I was "the *dumbest* smart guy" he knew. Everyone in class laughed. Coach meant that, while I made good grades, I lacked common sense. Head in the clouds, I tended to miss certain things.

One afternoon that year, I showed up for baseball practice in a downpour, having completely missed that it had already been canceled. Waiting for the school bus, I stood under an awning apart from the other kids. I was (and still am) a chronic eavesdropper, absorbed in nearby conversations. I recognized *my* bus only as it was pulling away, belching black smoke. By the time I'd hustled back through the rain into the gym in hopes of bumming a ride with an upperclassman, the school was deserted, loose-leaf paper blowing like tumbleweeds through the lobby.

Coach's office was upstairs, but to use his phone required admitting yet another spaced-out mistake. I had a quarter in my pocket since a slice of pizza at lunch had cost a buck seventy-five. The pay phone hung on the lobby wall in view of a life-sized picture of my high school's famous basketball hero of yesteryear. They called him Pistol Pete because he was an excellent shot on the hardwood. As far as I knew, no one remembered his misses.

I dialed home and listened to three-and-a-half rings, then slammed the receiver down in its cradle before our answering machine could click on. I wanted my quarter back. I slipped the silver back in my pocket. I could visualize the entire walk home stretching out in my mind, a little less than four miles to my door, rambling through a few back yards. I hefted my backpack onto both shoulders, instead of the usual one shoulder like the cool guys, and slunk into the drizzling afternoon feeling sorry for myself, the *dumbest*.

———❦———

My oldest son, Sam, does well in his prekindergarten assessment, identifying all the letters and numbers in a quiet, confident voice. His teacher smiles at me afterward and sing-songs above my child's head: "You know he's very bright, right?"

In the grocery store for a celebratory treat, my flesh and blood followed some flight of fancy in his head and floated away down the aisle while I was on the phone with a parishioner. Panic rising, I finally caught him sitting crisscross applesauce in the middle of Aisle 4 with a coloring book in his lap. And I thundered: "There you are! What were you thinking? You know better than to leave ... Are you listening, Son? Son! Pay attention!"

While in seminary, I learned Erik Erikson's stages of development, including the second stage of developing autonomy. The shadow side of autonomy is shame. Shame has no place in anything that is life-giving, including religion. And I think that what we say to children, especially the way we say it, has power to crack something deep inside them, a fissure that only widens over time until they are adults carrying broken pieces of their own selves in their fragile, beautiful hands.

───── ❧ ─────

When I was about Sam's age, my father offered a sermon illustration about an older man who meticulously fastened enough helium balloons to his chair that he actually floated over his neighborhood. He *flew* in a lawn chair! I have no idea how Dad was tying this to scripture, but think of how the mind so easily floats away. Next thing you know, you've missed something important.

At five years old—excuse me, five *and a half*—
Sam colors the back of the bulletin while I preach.
He's not interested in baseball. Perhaps he's too
young? He does line up all his Matchbox cars in
a straight row across a table top, just like I did at
his age. And, just like I did, he makes elaborate
rocket ships out of stacks of books, magazines,
pillows, pencils, blankets, wooden alphabet blocks,
flashlights, measuring tape, candlesticks, bits of
yarn, red plastic cups, dead batteries, watering
cans, and souvenir baseball caps. Our Crazy Creek
lawn chair serves as his cockpit. He'll perch there,
wearing a far-away look, floating through his
imagination. My father says his grandson has a rich
inner-life. I do worry that he might miss things.
Important things. I am a worrier.

———⌘———

My hometown is called the City of Oaks. As
a freshman trudging beneath those silent giants,
I was wrapped up inside my thoughts, worrying
about my baseball swing, worrying about the acne
on my cheeks, and *really* worrying about this girl
from church who had been acting like she didn't
even know me in the school hallways. Hefting
these anxieties in my mind, I'd traveled up and
down a few hills without even realizing it. But then
the most imposing climb lay dead ahead, a steep

incline past Jaycee Park and its dirt infields where I'd first learned to play.

My father was my first coach. I was ten years old. The hip-hop duo Kris Kross had released their hit single "Jump," and I tried to memorize the rapid-fire rap lyrics on the way to our games, rewinding the cassette tape over and over, riding shotgun as Dad drove. I wore #8 on my uniform just like Cal Ripken, Jr., and one better than the #7 worn by Mickey Mantle—Dad's boyhood hero. My batting stance was too wide, but no one could convince me otherwise. Especially not him. It is easy to disregard the coach's advice if he is your parent and, besides, Dad was a *pastor*. What did he know?

I labored past the old ballpark and then right at the traffic light at the top of the hill, veering into the shaded neighborhood that led to home. I fished the spare key from under the backdoor mat and, after dumping my backpack in the laundry room, guzzled two full glasses of water at the sink. I changed out of my sopping wet clothes, then dug into a big bowl of cereal at the kitchen table. The garage door flung open with a *bang* against the wall and my father burst into the kitchen. I froze with spoon raised to my mouth.

"There you are! Just where in God's name have you been? Why didn't you call home? Didn't you think that I would go and look for you? Just what the hell were you thinking?"

Dad kicked the cabinet underneath the kitchen sink, then hopped around, holding his smarting foot, cursing like a big leaguer.

―∞∞―

Anne Lamott claims that grace bats last. Now that I am a father, I do listen to Dad. Especially the gentle sermons he offers when we are taking in a baseball game with my younger brother. At the venerable sanctuary known as Wrigley Field, Dad once mused that it is the job of every adolescent to put his or her parents on trial. And, make no mistake about it, every caregiver will be found guilty, for we are all imperfect. Children will remember our faults, our mistakes, our anger. Our sins do not float away as if on helium balloons. Wounds leave scars.

"But you can tell a story about a scar, Andrew. And what you hope and pray," Dad continued, "is that your child will grant you pardon."

KEEPSAKE, PART 1

Ask, and it shall be given unto you.
—Matthew 7:7

I spent much of my youth and young adulthood devoted to the religion of baseball. My younger brother and I bonded over the sacramental elements of glove and bat, spending countless days pitching batting practice to one another and playing catch until the last light of evening. As adults, we remain committed disciples. John and I used to make a pilgrimage every summer, no matter where we lived, to the cathedral of a Major League stadium and congregate with our father over this sacred rite.

Now that I am the father of three young children, I take my kids to the local college game and they take in the large crowds with eyes wide. I am attempting to make converts out of these youngsters, but I confess that they never sit still in our seats. Our tickets are essentially a down payment on a giant tub of popcorn with unlimited free refills.

It is easier to give my little players free-range over the picnic area, knowing they will return to graze from the popcorn bucket a few handfuls at a time. We average a refill every two innings. Not that they ever eat all of it. Much of the popcorn will end up on the ground, either by honest mistake or gleeful dumping.

Dad joins us at the ballpark in order to keep another pair of eyes on the kids. My head will swivel away from them at the sharp crack of a bat, and I'll catch a fleeting glimpse of an infielder diving after a line drive. But what little of the game I watch is mostly in line at the concession stand. On my third trip during our most recent game, the star player blasted a homerun. As the crowd roared, I glanced back at my home team, hoping they'd caught the thrill of watching the ball soar like a rocket over the wall. As my father looked on, the kids had knelt on the concrete to offer popcorn to a half-dozen pigeons who were as fat and happy as smiling little Buddhas.

"You back again, huh?" The smiling popcorn vendor interrupted my thoughts. Tufts of his salt and pepper hair poked sideways from underneath his cap. I held up my empty container with a sheepish shrug. He tapped his index finger twice on his chin, meditatively. "I'm sure you got kids. If I had to guess, probably three of them." He reached across the counter for my empty tub.

"Well, you just remember that there's always more where that came from," he said while passing the refill back to me. He added with a wink, "All you have to do is ask."

———— ∞ ————

I am grateful that, over the years, my younger brother has traveled many miles to share time with our family. There were holidays when quality time made up for a lack of quantity time. But lately, I've been saddened by the fact that John has never attended a baseball game with my three children. The reasons, I believe, have to do with distance: the distance between North Carolina and New York, the distance between the liturgical calendar and the academic calendar, the distance between two different paths through life, and the terrible distance between the words "not" and "yet."

There are, of course, many ways to be healthy, happy, and whole. As adults, my brother and I have made different choices about careers and families. I don't expect him to follow in my footsteps back to North Carolina. But life sprints by in seconds, my children outgrow their shoes seemingly every other month, and I'll never get the chance to retrace these exact steps with my brother. This spring, my sons have learned to climb trees, play checkers, and swing a baseball bat. It hurts when they beg for the chance to show off their skills to their uncle. I can give them all the popcorn they ask for, but I can't give them that time. And it's hard to explain. My sons cannot imagine waking up without seeing their brother.

There is a photograph our father snapped of John and me, just the two of us on the beach when we were about four and six. I am marching across the sand, my eyes forward; John follows, gazing down so that he can step into my footprints. I'm not looking back at him. Perhaps I took it for granted that he was behind me. My younger brother had this photo framed for my college graduation, though he was across that Atlantic Ocean studying abroad in Paris at the time. He had already begun to blaze his own path. Now I look at this framed photo with new eyes. As an adult, have I taken *him* for granted?

I believe that the mystery of God's love is that, like free refills, there's always much more where that came from. But I know that much of what I want, much of what *I love,* is in limited supply. There is only so much time. Christian theology has the paradoxical concept of the kingdom of heaven as both here and not yet—time is both fulfilled and still to come. I try to remember what poet Tony Hoagland wrote about savoring a certain moment "with all of its muchness." Moments like a homerun or offerings to Buddha pigeons. Moments like receiving reassurance from a kind stranger or meditating upon an old picture. I keep memories of certain moments with my brother as precious gifts, and I pray that such muchness can carry us safely through the distance.

KEEPSAKE, PART 2

Am I my brother's keeper?
—Genesis 4:9

The year is 2015. It is a week before Christmas, and I tell my oldest son, "It is a big responsibility to be a big brother." I can speak with such authority because my brother, John, is twenty-five months younger than me. My three-year-old, Sam, stares at me blankly from across the room, then continues playing with the nativity scene strewn across the floor in a mishmash of sheep and shepherds and Magi because—sweet baby Jesus!—who has the time to set up and organize and *keep* such a scene organized when you have two young boys?

I have collapsed into the old armchair I have owned since seminary. My youngest son, Asa, is only a month and a couple of weeks in change and lies on a blanket at my feet gumming a wooden figurine of that awed and bewildered father in Bethlehem long ago. Sam points at the floor and asks, "Is that safe?" His brother babbles in tongues.

Later that evening, after my sons are safely in bed, my younger brother calls. I confirm that his gifts for his nephews have arrived in the mail and are now under our tree. I tell him another thing that Sam had said earlier that day: "Getting is good, but giving is *gooder*." We chuckle, then there's a lull in our conversation. I am standing in the silence, looking out the kitchen window up into the canopy of a giant oak tree. The branches have divided the night sky into a patchwork quilt, reminding me of the blanket John and I used to hide under as boys, making our own little world.

John likes to quote Walt Whitman: "Do I contradict myself? / Very well then I contradict myself, / I am large, I contain multitudes." I like to say that brothers speak a language of mind and might. Some of the vocabulary is actually fists and tears and broken bones; others are bike chains and baseball gloves and bear hugs completed with two thumps on the back. A mentor once told me those two back pats stand for "Love You."

When my younger brother first learned to walk, I would knock him down so often that he began to point his finger at me even when he fell on his own. He would wail: "An-new!" Growing up, he and I fought more times than I care to remember.

My only fistfight with someone other than John occurred during Christmas vacation in seventh grade on the blacktop of our old elementary school. A kid from out of town—visiting his sweet grandmother, for goodness' sake!—threw a basketball off my head and I swung at him. He came back with an expert right and a well-placed left and would have landed more blows save for my little brother throwing his kid body between us with a mighty scream.

My grownup brother now teaches math in a public high school. Shortly after my first son was born, I flew from my home in Virginia to New York City and tagged along to my brother's work. I wore a Visitor badge and sat in the front row. Dry erase marker in hand, my younger brother whirled from the whiteboard to call the name of a student in the back of the room. The student answered correctly, and John gave him a knowing smile.

Back at his tiny apartment, I presented John with an early Christmas gift: a small decorative bowl woven by a local artist out of lacquered magazine strips. I instructed him to keep the bowl by his door and empty his pockets there as soon as he came home, explaining that he would save precious time every morning if he didn't have to move heaven and earth to find his keys and stuff. I could tell he almost rolled his eyes. But we exchanged a hug. Two back pats.

We attended many a lock-in as middle schoolers in our father's church. Orchestrated for the youth by our adult leaders, these overnight events involved food, games, movies, and very little sleep, curled up in sleeping bags scattered across the floor of the fellowship hall, the girls on one side and we boys on the other. My first crush was on this girl who brought cigarettes to one of these lock-ins. She showed me the tip of the pack peeking out of the back pocket of her jeans. Pizza and the first movie were followed by Bible study and the second movie. Finally, she and I snuck away and lit up on the front steps of the sanctuary—the same place Dad greeted parishioners after pronouncing the benediction. We did not smoke as much as cough and gag. But we kept at it, cool as we were.

Eventually we stumbled inside, high on nicotine and the forbidden. John was the only one still awake.

"Whew! Buddy, you stink!"

He blew into the opening of a Styrofoam cup of hot chocolate. I asked him why he called me "Buddy" because he had never done that before.

"You just don't seem like Andrew right now."

———— ∞∞ ————

This year, during my search and rescue mission for Christmas decorations from the dungeon we know as the basement—among all the dusty spider webs, snake skins, exiled children's toys (most of which play music) and God-only-knows what else—I happened upon my old skateboard. A painted Snoopy still smiled beneath his cool sunglasses. I flipped John's gift over onto its grimy wheels and coasted only a few feet.

But in that short distance, I was transported to the heady time of seminary more than ten years ago. After studying all afternoon, I'd finally admit to myself that I'd been reading the same circuitous paragraphs over and over without the slightest comprehension. I'd leave the library through the double glass doors and hit the fresh air. Once free, I would then coast around the flat rectangle of the quad's dormant winter grass. An outside boy, once again, skateboarding among the trees, obscure theological words left behind.

John still teaches in the Big Apple. He doesn't go to church. I don't think he'll ever understand why I want to give so much of my time and energy to what he considers a problematic, hypocritical institution. I am not blind to the contradictions between what Christians say and do, especially in comparison to the teachings of the One we follow. But I think of the church as large, containing multitudes among all those contradictions. And yet I still care deeply about how I appear in my brother's eyes.

So I have kept that skateboard all these years, because when I was in seminary, the real gift was having something fun to talk about with him: How was my riding? Was I learning any tricks? We'd laugh like kids again. Maybe that's the secret.

III

SCREAMS AND
SONGS

You've got yesterday, today, and tomorrow
all in the same room ...
—Bob Dylan

SALTED COFFEE

Bleary-eyed, I watch my beloved slip
two spoonfuls of salt into her coffee,
realizing her mistake at first sip. And a
scream bursts from her lips, the pent-up
frustration born from a night of rising
too many times to nurse, flinging back
the covers each time with a mumbled
curse. Before our three kids multiplied
our lives, we vowed to become two into
one. Biblical math is a mystery, yet we
count the costs: one checking, one
mortgage, one deductible. Dinner dates
we count on our fingers. Two hands
plus two hands equals a division of
labor. One to cook, one to clean, one to
change the diaper and one to chase the
other two. Pain is loud, though the daily
sounds can deafen you to each other
until one happens to salt the coffee.
And a scream becomes our prayer of
illumination, the dawning that in coupling,
there must be a you, too.

WHIMSY

He moves your bones, and the way is clear.
—Wendell Berry

His name was Drew, and he was not my alter ego. More like a phase for a few years after college.

I'd always been called "Andrew" by adults, never "Drew" (or "Andy" for that matter) until my junior year of undergrad. The guys on the baseball team and later the fraternity dudes all called me by my last name—Troutman. Trout or Trouty, for short. But this young woman I began to date gave me the pet name "Drew" on a whim, and it stuck for almost five years.

The first thing to note about Drew was his long hair—thick and curly. Like a shrubbery. Fraternity brothers had other nicknames for him: Ronald McDonald and Sideshow Bob. Drew worshipped Bob Dylan and sung his own god-awful poetry to basic guitar chords: "Well, the words reside deep inside / get faded away by the look in her eyes / that melts away my alibis / so why ask why."

Not completely oblivious, Drew submitted to the barber upon graduation to prepare for a job interview as a youth director at a Presbyterian church. When they hired him, Drew grew back his bushy curls. He wore sandals on his feet and a haphazard beard on his face. On Sundays, his wrinkled clothes held the shape of sleep. Later, after a mission trip to the Appalachian Mountains, Drew always wore around his neck a piece of dirty string from which hung a penny.

For that mission trip, Drew had drummed up participation from about twenty high school students and secured six adult volunteers. To keep himself organized, he'd color-coded a system of files for all medical records, permission slips, and waiver forms. Finally, on a Saturday morning, as all joined hands in a circle, Drew was the one who led the prayer. Then he drove one of the rented fifteen-passenger vans.

As the caravan moved west, rolling slopes gradually crested into mountain peaks. Gas stations began to double as restaurants, their signs advertising petroleum, hamburger plates, and live bait. Drew drove past dozens and dozens of churches: white clapboard Methodist churches with sturdy steeples, brick Baptist churches with stained glass windows, and the tiniest buildings bearing the longest names—*Washed in the Blood and Born in the Spirit Holiness Church. Jesus is the*

Solid Rock Church of God. Holy Refuge Pentecostal Fire Missionary Temple.

Bushy hair bouncing, Drew revved the mechanical beast loaded with high schoolers up the holler, past frantic chickens and smudge-faced toddlers wearing nothing more than adult T-shirts down past their knobby knees. They had arrived. And Drew was ready to work.

Over the course of that week, Drew instructed, cajoled, begged, and inspired his students to paint, nail, clean, and saw. They all slept in a gym. There was one afternoon off, and they swam in a cold mountain pond. The true baptism, however, was by fire. As wood chips and screws flew, as Band-Aids and spackle were affixed, the students built themselves into a team, helping one another hang siding, patch roofs, and construct steps. There was sweat, Gatorade, bologna and cheese, laughter, and most of all, love. Real love, not the warm fuzzies plastered on Hallmark cards, but love like the mountain man who emerged from the depths of the dark trailer at the end of the week.

His name was Ralph and, in addition to his pride, he wore a thick red beard. On the last day, Ralph said the new back steps for his home made him happier than a tiny bird in a little house. And he showed Drew his electric guitar and how to play the solo on Pink Floyd's "Wish You Were Here," an experience that Drew knew he would never forget even as the notes faded from his fingertips.

On the last night in the mountains, Drew drilled holes in the pennies and gave the necklaces to the students in hopes that they might take something with them, remembering how small gestures can be priceless.

Back in the suburbs, Drew searched in vain for the same mountaintop experience. He began to allow middle schoolers to pile into his dad's Camry and blast punk rock until the speakers blew. This meant that Drew drove around for the rest of the year listening to Jack Johnson from a small boombox because he couldn't afford new speakers. He had student loans to pay and was saving up to buy an engagement ring for the young woman who'd given him his nickname.

His fiancée-to-be was still a couple of years from finishing her degree. Upon her graduation, she and Drew were to be married and have two children, maybe more. Their marriage was never in question...until it was.

During college, Drew used to stop by her dorm just to hear the song of her voice. Now, after graduation, he was beginning to resent her nightly nagging phone call, her chitter about her sorority, her impatience with the details of his ministry. It wasn't only the two-hour drive that separated them; there were the ever-widening gaps between college and what you might call the real world, between the church and what you might call the secular world. Life in college was not as much carefree as it was care-forward—cares like bills and insurance and debts were, for privileged kids like them, a reality postponed and relegated to "The Future." But Drew had arrived at his future, while she was still living in her care-forward present.

Years before, she'd nicknamed him on a lark. *That* Drew, *her* Drew, used to pick dogwood blossoms from trees and tuck them behind her ear. But when Drew started working for the church, she told him that being a youth director wasn't a "real job." Whimsy had lost its charm. Drew felt certain ministry was a real, deliberate, and thoughtful calling.

After The Break-Up, a couple of Drew's parishioners tried to set him up with their college-aged daughters. Bushy-haired, unshaven, wrinkled-clothes-wearing Drew found himself seated in an elaborate formal dining room before a place setting with many, *many* forks and one perfectly delightful young woman trying to make conversation across the towering silver candlesticks. On another occasion, Drew was set up with an intelligent and sophisticated young woman named Nikki. Upon their introduction, Drew lit up for the first time in a long while—that was the same name as his puppy! Drew quickly learned that this was not the right thing to say.

The puppy came into Drew's life as a gift from his fellow staff members at church, women who recognized Drew's heartache and knew there were no shortcuts to love. The afterschool director had found the dog abandoned by the side of the road, and the preschool director paid the vet for her shots. Drew named his new companion after his favorite poet, Nikki Giovanni, who had lectured at his alma mater years ago and had told the audience that everyone has at least one book to write, a promise Drew held onto when he was feeling really low.

After his girlfriend dumped him, when Drew was lying in bed with the shades drawn or crawling into a jug of cheap wine, little Nikki would lick his face. If that failed to rouse him, she would nip his toes. Out on their walks, they would crisscross the park, as Drew had to keep steering Nikki away from the fresh goose poop. This is how Drew made it through the dark winter and interminable spring without his girlfriend.

At long last, the next summer mission trip was only two weeks away. Drew held the last meeting for the students and chaperones. When everyone had left, following a whim, Drew decided to peek into the sanctuary. There was a healing and wholeness ceremony already underway.

The sanctuary was darkened and candlelit. Even a breath seemed to echo. Drew felt a shard of panic: What was going on here? He sat quietly in the last pew on the left, thinking he could always escape unnoticed. A couple handfuls of people were singing a slow refrain. Scriptures were offered, familiar stories of Jesus and healing. Then worshippers were invited into a time of silent prayer.

Though he prayed publicly, such as after the youth meeting, Drew had fallen out of the habit of private practice. His girlfriend had prayed and, when she finally told him that she wouldn't marry him, he had stopped praying as a way to distance himself from her, though he didn't realize it. Down the corridor of time, this seems like taking rat poison and expecting it to kill the critter under the couch. But grief is not rational. This is why puppies are such good therapists.

At the healing and wholeness service, Drew remained seated as the last song ended and people rose from the pews to walk reverently forward to receive the laying on of hands. He checked his watch: nearly eight o'clock. He had to get home to let Nikki outside. Whispers came in waves, rising and falling from the lay leaders gathered up front. Looking up from his watch, Drew happened to see a single candle wink out. Smoke rose like a winding mountain road, and Drew realized that he, too, was actually walking forward, heading toward a church member he recognized but barely knew, an older woman with no connection to the youth group. She was smiling, gently and humbly, like a saint or a bodhisattva or a child.

Now, everything was soft and muted, even the wooden floor under his knees. Now, this woman's hand was on top of Drew's head with surprising strength that made him hold his breath. Now, she began to pray heavy words, deliberately measured between thick silences. And as the words dripped upon him, Drew began to feel warmth, beginning on the top of his head, then rolling like molasses down his neck and spreading across his shoulders. That's when Drew's shoulders began to shake.

Drew sobbed in great waves that rose in his chest and broke from his mouth. This sobbing seemed like an eternity to him. Through the fog of his anguish, Drew gradually became aware of more hands on his head, their heat like glowing coals. Still he wept and wailed, sputtered and shook, gasped and groaned until, finally, he seemed washed out like an ancient river bed. Only then did he lift his head. The woman had candlelight in her eyes.

"Ah-*men*," she emphasized.

Drew drove back to his little apartment, hardly aware of the journey until he had arrived. Once outside, Nikki began to bark at the door of the Camry. Following her lead, Drew opened the door, and she leaped into the backseat, tail wagging. She continued to bark.

"Let's *go*," she seemed to say.

As Drew drove west with the windows down, Bob Dylan's *Blood on the Tracks* was his traveling mercy. Nikki fell asleep in the back, her head on her paws. Drew drove and drove. He drove until he reached the dark mountains. Only then did he stop to refuel, fishing enough change from the ashtray for a large coffee for him and a hot dog for his dog. Drew pulled back into the apartment complex as the first light of dawn began winking above the horizon.

There were many more weary days ahead. But following another whim, Drew enrolled in a few online classes at the seminary. Then, in a simple twist of fate, he met a young woman at a cookout who, for some reason, gave him a high-five after their introduction. She had a brother named Drew.

So I was back to "Andrew" that very evening, two years before I married her.

MY MOST SELFISH PRAYER

For Ginny, of course

I'm bouncing our baby daughter on my lap as she drools on a wooden rattle. Her mom makes pancakes every Saturday morning, but the baby has only recently gotten her first taste. Our middle child, age two *and a half*—his big brother has taught him to *emphasize*—marks time by the weekly passage of pancakes, which doesn't seem all *that* idolatrous to me.

My wife and I are both ordained. But she alone is the Saturday priest, the celebrator of this eucharist of flour, butter, and syrup. Her sacred ingredients include bananas and coconut oil. With an expert flick of the spatula, she flips a perfect circle of golden deliciousness while humming a beautiful nothing. Music mixes with aromas in the air and I know, *I know*, this will not last forever.

O Lord, let me die before my wife.

I'm quick to add something like, "Dear Lord, may she and I enjoy many, *many* pancakes in a long, *long* future together."

O may it be so.

———✸———

My wife knows that I would like the hymn "What Wondrous Love Is This" to be sung at the service of witness to the resurrection after my death.

> *What wondrous love is this,*
> *O my soul, O my soul ...*
> *And when from death I'm free,*
> *I'll sing and joyful be ...*

I know she will cry there in the sanctuary. I pray that our three adult children will be there to hold her. They would never try to shush her— "There, there, Mom"—because she has encouraged them to cry their whole lives. She teaches all of us that our greatest strength is our vulnerability, our child-like faith.

O may there be beautiful and brilliant grandchildren clustered around her knees, living testaments to a parabolic truth uttered long ago that "of such as these is the kingdom of heaven." O may my beloved cradle a great-grandchild in her arms! She can smell that baby's head, the scent a wordless prayer rising like incense or hymns or the smell of pancakes.

———ɶɞ———

I have been by her side as she birthed three children. Over the course of our ministries, she and I have been in dozens of Hospice rooms. There are obvious differences between deathbeds and deliveries, yes. And yet I am always struck by the similarities: how all the attention is upon the one in the bed, making sure she is comfortable—not understanding what it is *like*, mind you, but trying to be as supportive as you possibly can. How there is *a lot* of prayer, both spoken and unspoken. How there is often cursing, and sometimes how cursing is prayer. How time stalls and starts, then stops ... and somehow starts again. How there is wonder and pain, fear and hope. How the end might not be always in sight, but the end is always in mind. How love never ends.

I've never forgotten how a midwife whispered through one of my wife's fearsome contractions, "Trust him coming into the world." It seems to me that a person has some say as to the exact moment when he or she leaves this world. Some seem to wait for a loved one to arrive, others for a loved one to leave. I've seen the sun break through clouds and snow begin to fall at those precise moments of parting. It's amazing and painful and graceful how many people die at sunrise or sunset.

I don't so much care about the time of day, as I only want her to be holding my hand.

O may it be so.

———❦———

She has been known to say that she will die first. Early in our marriage, I chuckled this away, being in the afterglow of the adolescent illusion of immortality. After the recent funeral service for my uncle, my wife repeated her prediction on the drive home. Children were asleep in the minivan; the only sound was that of empty juice boxes rattling around on the floor. I just nodded. And silently prayed otherwise. O Lord, let me die before my wife.

Being in the ministry has taught me that a widow or widower will take up birding or biking or cooking or cards. If healthy, travel the country— even the world. If sickly, spend time alone in nature or in poetry, perhaps tending begonias or to Dickinson's couplets. Evenings are the hardest, most say. That immense emptiness of a bedroom where one partner is gone forever. So, they take to rockers on the front porch or in the lobby of the assisted living facility, and most are grateful for company. I have talked of the weather, shared the Eucharist, and then talked about the possibility of different weather. People claim to spend a lot of time in bed and yet apologize for their tiredness. I have witnessed how easily the tears appear at the most subtle reminders of loss, like a bag of peanuts or a distant train whistle or a seemingly innocuous word like "sunrise." For those left behind, the sun, rising and setting, simply illuminates that lonely road.

———————

And when from death I'm free,
I'll sing and joyful be,
And through eternity,
I'll sing on, I'll sing on ...

While I really don't think she'll be able to "sing and joyful be" at my funeral, I would hope to bring her a little joy from beyond the veil. Are spouses clamoring in The Beyond to get double rainbows placed in perfect view of their surviving partners? In timelessness, do you still have to wait in line? Is there a cap on heavenly signs allotted to individual souls? How about the flick of an angel wrist to cause a pancake to appear in the shape of a heart? And what about blue herons?

When we were struggling with infertility, she and I used to take long walks by the New River. Once a blue heron soared into flight just as we rounded a bend. Its broad, beating wings were a sign to us of coming life. Could I make another heron happen for her in my life after life?

Life After Life is the title of a well-known book that chronicles the testimonies of clinically dead people who were then resuscitated. Across cultures and religions, people have described almost exactly the same occurrences: a lifting from the body into a dark tunnel above. But there is no fear. Only a bright, warm light visible at the far end. And a presence—not a person exactly—but someone familiar in the light at the end of the tunnel, perhaps waiting to usher the deceased into ... where? What exactly? What wondrous love is this?

——⊗⊗⊗——

I would also like for the famous Thirteenth Chapter of First Corinthians to be read at the service of witness to the resurrection after my death. This gorgeous declaration of enduring love was not a part of our marriage ceremony. We were married in our seminary's chapel, which is round, lacking a center aisle. It was her idea that we would both enter with our parents from opposite ends and meet in the middle. The processional began, and I *hustled* forward. Mom on one arm and Dad on the other, I was all but dragging my parents in tow. We rounded the first pew ahead of her ...

My wife's *energy* came around the bend and met us before she did. There was an oncoming force, as palpable to me as it was invisible. And it was *her*. Or, some part of her. The Her of her. In that moment, all other sounds and sights and awareness faded away, and all I knew was that I *knew* she was coming to me.

I'll go first. And then, once again, may she come to me.

O may it be so.

EXPOSURE

Numb the dark and you numb the light.
—Brené Brown

My sweet Sadie, as your mom and I planned and prepared for your birth, we dreamed about those first few moments with you. I imagined your soft breath upon my face. Your tiny fist curled around my pointer finger. Your little warm body on my chest, skin-to-skin. I envisioned that the first words you would hear outside the womb would be your name followed by "I love you."

Immediately after you came into the world, a nurse whooped, "You the *cheesiest* girl I ever seen!"

You, our dear toddler, are indeed cheesy sometimes, sporting your silly grin and your dimples that go on for days. Your mom says that you get your goofiness from me. But, of course, that's not what this nurse meant. She delighted in your "cheesiness" because you were born with a particularly thick layer of cheese-like *vernix caseosa* coating your delicate skin. This sticky, white substance kept you warm and dry in your little sea of amniotic fluid and prevented attacks from certain bacteria. Your "cheese" was your first armor.

Now, as I imagine your growing to become a woman like your mother and the mothers who came before her, I can't help but wish sometimes that you still had another layer of protection. I'll give you things, like sunscreen, to protect you from harsh physical exposure. But I wish you might also be shielded from another kind—from the double-standards and double-binds, from "damned-if-you-do, damned-if-you-don't." What can I offer to shield you from sexism celebrated in the workplace and inequality sacralized by the church?

As you grow, your mom and I will strive to keep you safe. But to be born is to be exposed. To become vulnerable is scary, and yet it also affords the opportunity to make discoveries about yourself. Remember that one meaning of "exposure" relates to photography, to the light allowed on a camera lens. While we cannot always protect you from the world, your mom and I can give you ways to view yourself, to bring the picture into focus. The right exposure brings clarity to both shadows and light. Allow me to share a few pictures with words ...

You, Sadie, are named after your mom's great-grandmother. She was strong and able, mowing her grass until the week she died. She was also strong-willed. Your great-great-grandmother did not suffer fools gladly. And she was strongly committed to her faith. She died sitting in her easy chair on a Sunday morning, waiting for a friend to take her to church.

Decades later, right after you were born, several nurses started wiping off your cheesy layer of protection, and your booming cries resounded in the room. The same nurse spoke again.

"Will you listen to her? She's *strong*."

Maybe somewhere your great-great-grand–mother smiled, approvingly. Who knows?

My favorite story about your namesake is that she gave a certain great-granddaughter aluminum tins to make mud pies in her backyard—a little indulgence that left a lasting impression on your mom. Who knows what strength and grace your great-great-grandmother has passed down to you?

You, Sadie Anna, are also named after my mom. Your Nana knows that this world, fully exposed, is full of beauty and pain, injustice and mercy. An avid student of Brené Brown's book *Daring Greatly*, your Nana believes that to be exposed is to become vulnerable, and to become vulnerable is a faithful act of courage.

From the time you were born, your Nana has told you, "It is holy to know what you want." She has traveled the world. She will tell you that she is a pilgrim, a woman who seeks the holy in different places and the faces of other people. Who knows what courage she will inspire in you?

My sweet Sadie, you do indeed get your cheesiness from me. The color of your eyes comes from your mom. Like her, your eyes are bright blue. We keep a picture of your mom as a little girl in your nursery. Mom is probably three years old, blue eyes shining as she rides her red tricycle. And she reaches out with her left hand as if she knows exactly what she wants. Will you listen to her? She's strong. Strong enough to be vulnerable.

As you seek to bring the picture of your life into focus, I want you to know and be inspired by a strong and courageous story from the day you were born. As your mom groaned through a particularly fierce contraction, her doula pulled a stool behind her to massage her shoulders, and the birth photographer slipped behind the doula to rub her neck, and the midwife stood behind the photographer to massage her shoulders. That contraction seemed endless. Yet those women kept their strong hands upon one another until, finally, that fearsome contraction passed. There were more to come, but in that pregnant pause, all four broke into cheesy smiles. Your mom actually giggled, "Don't we make a picture?"

Sixteen months later, you beep-bop around the house, toddling along to some joyful melody only you can hear. If you catch someone watching, you'll pause and say with a grin, "Cheese!" In this way, "cheese" is still your protection, not as an armor, but in the way your smile lets in the light. And I can only add, "Amen."

PEEKING

Something about this slanting
morning light
reminds me
how he looked for you,
peeking around the corner
into our kitchen.

I can see how he was in it,
eyebrows arched, cheeks flushed,
smile brimming on his lips,
"Ma-ma" on the tip of his tongue.

How he looked for you,
peeking around the corner
every single morning.

We rarely peek with the faith of a child.

Change is the only constant,
we learn soon enough.
You and I are never the same
in any angled light.

Yet every single morning
I want to be illuminated
by how he looked for you.

COMMA, LOVE

Once in a while we should gently say what is.
—Brian Doyle

At my favorite coffee shop, I was taking a mid-afternoon sabbath, savoring the pause in my busy day to enjoy a quiet moment. My coffee was steaming and dark. The scone before me was buttery and soft with little treasures of cranberries buried beneath the surface. And the people-watching—*exquisite*.

Take the guy with the cryptic tattoo on the back of his neck. There were swirls of dark blue like Van Gogh's starry night erupting from his collar, rising all the way up to his ears. As I stared at the design, wondering if a hidden picture might suddenly appear like one of those Magic Eye posters, I overheard a young woman a couple tables over loudly exclaim to her friend, "And I told my husband like, *comma*, you just don't get it!"

What exactly was not gotten I will never know; after that, she dropped her voice to a whisper. But I was amazed by what I'd heard—the vocalized comma! Not just a pause, but a deliberate verbalization of a pause. It was marvelous, an explicit recognition of a moment of intense feeling that was worth stopping for, however briefly.

The young women went out into the sunshine, eventually followed by the indecipherable neck tattoo, but I continued to sit and stir and ponder.

───·∞∞·───

I read scripture from the pulpit on Sunday mornings. Some of my favorite verses make excellent use of the comma: "Who will separate us from the love of Christ? Will hardship, or distress, or persecution, or famine, or nakedness, or peril, or sword?" Each time one of these disasters is mentioned, the comma heightens the tension. I think the comma helps us to "get it" by asking us to slow down. "No, in all these things, we are more than conquerors through him who loved us." A comma is shaped like a cresting wave, and then we get the conclusion like the crashing surf. Despite all our rising insecurities, we don't have to be anxious, being secure in love like an ocean in our souls.

Wedding vows also make excellent use of the comma, as in "to have and to hold, from this day forward, for better, for worse, for richer, for poorer, in sickness and in health." These commas are of course unvocalized, not spoken. The gentle pauses between the words are my favorite part of attending a wedding. Because, in the comma moments, I remember my own bride, standing before me, her hands in mine, and how there was a light in her face as she repeated our vows.

I also remember a particular ceremony I officiated when, as part of their vows, the couple recited the Thirteenth Chapter of First Corinthians. In unison. From memory. This was entirely the bride's idea and I had tried to talk her out of it. Seems like a lot of pressure to put on yourself. You want to be in the moment, not in your head! Wouldn't it be better for me just to read it? She was adamant. The groom and I relented.

When it came time for the First Corinthians moment, the bride and groom turned to face one another, held hands, then locked eyes. She nodded, and they began the recitation in lockstep, enunciating each word as a single trail of footprints. Soon enough, the groom stumbled and fell behind half a pace. I still can hear how she gently paused between the words, allowing him to catch up. The words were about love, but I heard the power of love in the pauses.

"Love is, patient. Love is, kind."

Recently, Ginny and I attended a family wedding. My wife's nephew is four years old and attends a Christian preschool. He used to be so quiet! Now, he asks questions like, how come God created mosquitoes? Mosquitoes make you itch, he explained. Itching is bad. God is good. So, why did God create them? He looked at me, unblinking.

"Well," I stammered, "it's like," then my six-year-old son rushed up with toy tractors and the boys were off. I was saved by the comma.

During this wedding, however, I did not get to rest in the pauses. Due to a thunderstorm, the ceremony was moved indoors, specifically to a barn. A few minutes into the processional, the sweat beads were processing down my back like the bridesmaids down the aisle. Not only that, but our youngest son, Asa, had discovered the dirt on the floor and was mucking around, pretending to be a bulldozer in his good church clothes. My wife whispered, fiercely: *"Take him out of here!"* No commas, and I did not waste time.

Outside the barn, there was fresh air and the faint whine of mosquitoes. Eventually, I heard the cheers. "That's for the kiss," I told my son. "Now, they're married!" And he paused in his playing to look up at me, grinning widely. Soon enough, he went back to making piles out of the gravel in the parking lot. He was a hot mess, but that look on his cherub face!

Later, during the reception, I had the chance to shake the pastor's hand. Before I had to leave the ceremony, I caught the beginning of his homily, and I especially appreciated the story from the bride's youth, how she had skipped down the carpeted aisle of her home church to answer the call to Jesus. Today, the pastor observed, she had come down another aisle with equal joy. I loved how he deftly connected those two stories. Beautiful, poignant, and holy. Stories really are prayers of terrific power.

The pastor smiled by way of accepting my appreciation. Then, a far-off look came to his eyes: "Time, it sure does fly."

Silently, I smiled, too. But to myself, I was like, comma, I get it.

I SING ASA

There is a healer in this house.
—Bry Webb

O ur middle child is named Asa, which means "healer" in Hebrew. His biblical namesake was the fifth ruler in the House of David, the third king of Judah. In his three and a half years, our Asa has had more days with a royally runny nose than without. (His big brother passes down everything from T-shirts to germs.) On any given day, chances are high that Asa's nose will be dripping with what I call "The Slimer"—a green, gelatinous glob like the lovable yet disgusting character from *Ghostbusters*. Asa will hold still only long enough for me to smear the ectoplasm across his cheeks, leaving a stickiness that will later collect dirt, graham cracker crumbs, and strawberry pulp.

Our Asa recently went over the handlebars on his balance bike and surfed the asphalt on his top lip. But by the evening bath, our child named Healer was already proud of his "boo-boos," pointing them out to his baby sister. The thirteenth-century poet Rumi claimed that your wound is the place where the light enters you. Healing, then, takes many forms.

———⊶∞⊷———

When asked what he wants to be when he grows up, Asa replies with utmost seriousness, "Lion."

He loves to play doctor, toting his plastic medical toys in his little green bag, then checking your reflexes with a swift karate chop to your knee. A moment later, he is a firefighter, racing through the kitchen shouting siren noises. Occasionally, Asa is Pastor Pete, scrawling his sermons in crayon.

More often, Asa calls himself Mail-Mail Pete. Fishing an imaginary key from his back pocket, he pretends to crank the ignition on his scooter—his Mail-Mail Truck—before kicking off down the sidewalk. He skitters to a stop at a neighbor's front step, lobbing an imaginary package onto the porch. Mister Rogers, a fellow Presbyterian pastor, claimed that play is really the work of childhood, for children pretend in order to comprehend their true identities. Our Healer is a true giver, a generous heart.

But the shadow side to Asa's imagination occurs in the middle of the night. Sometimes he cries out in terror. He'd been dreaming of a big brown dog in his bed or a bunch of gray spiders coming down onto his face. He tells me these details as I hold him in the bottom bunk. My hand is upon his chest, and I can feel his heart *thump-thump-thumping* as through a stethoscope.

Middle children often have to compete for their caregivers' attention. Think Jan Brady: "Marsha, Marsha, *Marsha!*" As his sister began to crawl and his brother started school, our middle child commenced hurling all the pillows off the couch and dumping all the Tinker Toys down the stairs. Without warning, he'd pour out all his milk onto the table and then chuck the glass, dashing it against the floor into a thousand shards. Recently, Asa colored his belly button so dark that, even though this marker was washable, it took several days for his skin to return to normal. Even more damage has been inflicted upon his siblings. While King Asa ruled Judah for forty-one years of relative peace and prosperity, our own little kingdom occasionally spirals into nightmarish chaos by Asa's hands. He bounced a hefty rock off his brother's head and a knot swelled up like a weather balloon. He crawled under the table and bit his baby sister's foot, leaving a half-circle of tiny bruises after the teeth marks faded. He slapped his mother in the face. I roared, "Asa, Asa, *Asa!*"

In the Gospels, women and men implore Jesus for healing. "Your faith has made you well," Jesus often responded. Whether born in the middle or not, we must find a middle ground between independence and dependence, knowing when to press forward on our own and when to ask for help.

His fist thrust into the air like a little king, Asa's favorite exclamation is, "I do it myself!" Our middle child can pour his own cereal. He can put on his own rain boots. He can use the potty by himself (I am quick to thank the Lord God Almighty for this grace). Bystanders watch in awe as Asa zips by on his scooter with one leg hanging Zen-like in the air, his wide grin flashing past. He climbs by himself to the top of the playground. Years ago, I probably would have held his older brother's hands down the slide. But Asa careens down a winding slide, landing on his bottom with a *thump* into the mulch. He gets up and brushes himself off, grinning brightly. His mother is so good about saying, "Asa, you must feel proud right now."

Asa will sprint down the street making siren noises (he is Fireman Pete) until his little legs can go no farther. Out of breath, he'll then utter his own unique construction: "Carry you me." I'll happily scoop him up and recall the song "Asa" by Bry Webb, in which the father sings to his son: "Let the shadows grow / to the end of the road / I will carry you home."

In Webb's song and my Asa's sweet request, I am reminded of the biblical metaphor for grace:

It is the good shepherd who carries the lost lamb home (Matt. 18:12–14).

———— ∞ ————

King Asa did depose the Queen Mother, Maacah, from her place in the royal court because she had made an idol dedicated to a fertility goddess (2 Chron. 15:16). Oh, the irony! Granted, the kings of Israel are known to rise, or fall, based on their absolute loyalty to the Lord God. King Asa must have felt proud in tearing down the idols in the high places—but did he have to be so hard on his mama?

Our Asa walks in his mother's footsteps. Ginny is athletic, a high school varsity letter winner in three sports. She's at home in her body and good with her hands. In Myers-Briggs terms, part of her personality is Sensing (S), meaning she focuses on physical realities like sights, sounds, tastes, and smells. She is attuned with what is present and real. As a girl, she had the same favorite sentence: "I do it myself."

Asa and his mom have the most expressive faces I've ever seen. There's never any doubt what my loves are thinking. And they also have the same fire! Our middle child's destructive ways toward glassware and siblings cause his mother's nostrils to flare and, later in private, she'll utter a string of obscenities that would make dear Fred Rogers blush.

I find comfort from Jesus's promise to be present when two or three are gathered. Most often, I've heard this passage cited at small gatherings, say, a new Bible study. Uttered with a shrug or even a sigh, the implication is that numbers are not *that* important. But right after pledging to bring the lost sheep back to the fold, Jesus promises to be in the middle of disagreements among members of the same church family (Matt. 18:12–20).

Several verses in the New Testament identify Christ as the mediator—the one in the middle. I think of a mediator settling a dispute. Such a person is outside the conflict. A mediation may result in a gracious separation. But I believe Christ to be love incarnate—in the middle of our pain and brokenness. The work of love is reconciliation, often painful, yet ultimately unifying.

One afternoon I came home for a late lunch and found the house strangely quiet. Our baby was napping. Asa was half-asleep in his mother's lap, a book of wild animals open before them on the bedroom floor. Not wishing to disturb them, I silently watched her reading from the door. Asa noticed me first. "Daddy, come read with us." I sat down on the floor next to my wife. "No, Daddy. Closer, sit *closer.*" He snuggled in so that he balanced on both of our laps. And the world melted away, the extraordinary right in the middle of the ordinary.

—∞∞∞—

Our middle child is an early riser. I'm usually awake, drinking coffee and writing. As Intuitive (N), I tend to focus on the big picture, as well as the future. But I am present enough to answer Asa's summons to the bedroom so that my nursing wife can rest as long as our baby permits it. Big Brother rolls over in the top bunk, settling back in. I take Asa for a walk through the dawn light. Being in the middle affords us this special time together.

Asa sits in the stroller, a bowl of cereal in his lap, naming things he sees. Fire hydrant. Squirrel. Minivan. He pops a piece of cereal into his mouth. While he chews, my mind begins to ruminate upon what I am supposed to do today and the upcoming water bill and the cryptic response I received from a visitor after Sunday's sermon and ... Asa calls me back to the present: "Oh, look! There's a rabbit! He is a Daddy Rabbit!"

He reminds me once again of Bry Webb's song: "Let your errands wait / until tomorrow / carry on and play / let the day be long."

After our stroll, Asa—excuse me—Mail-Mail Pete dons his helmet. Then he climbs on his scooter, ahem, Mail-Mail Truck, and coasts down the sidewalk. The day looms ahead, including its difficulties, trials, and pains. There are conflicts to negotiate. Forgiveness and reconciliation to work toward until the shadows lengthen and the evening comes. But, now, Asa looks back over his shoulder.

Our Healer laughs, and I sing Asa.

AFTERWORD

A Father's Advice to Himself

Don't worry. The tooth fairy knows this beach house.
She will put a starfish under your son's pillow.
When he wakes, his tongue wiggling in the hole,
dream she flew through a crack in the window.
And when he wonders, over the cereal bowl,
if she knows Santa and his eight reindeer,
consider how they all might vacation together,
might even be here for all we know!

Notice every beautiful nothing, and
make his world magic as best you can.
Put on your swimsuits, walk down to the sand.
Trail behind, step in his footprints and listen,
when he holds the conch shell to your ear,
Daddy, it's a walkie-talkie with the ocean.

ACKNOWLEDGEMENTS

Thank you to the Turnbulls at Light Messages for your faith and patience. Throughout the process of bringing this book to print, I have held onto Wally's delightful comment that this is the kind of book that is a privilege to publish.

In acknowledging that portions of this slender manuscript were first published elsewhere, I also wish to sing the praises of those women and men who have been a part of the journey. As Brian Doyle once e-mailed me, "I figure we are all a big chortling inky clan."

I am cheerfully indebted to my professor Laura Hope-Gill for her assurances that, despite my protests, I was a poet.

Versions of the poems "Beholden," "The Verbs of Them," and "Peeking" were published by *Bearings Online*, and I wish to thank Stina Kielsmeier-Cook and Susan Sink for their votes of confidence, as well as their editorial insights.

"Sundays From Now" was first published in *Time of Singing,* a grace-filled journal of Christian poetry edited by Lora Zill.

Versions of the essays "Inside Out Boys" and "Daffodils" as well as the poem that became "Grace Dance" first appeared in *The Presbyterian Outlook.* Thanks to Jana Blazak for her patience with my intuitive use of commas, and my tendency to unfortunately split infinitives. In addition, Jill Duffield convened a writing group that generated an early draft of "Spills" and I'm grateful for this holy opportunity with these wonderful writers and friends: Nannette Banks, Carlton Johnston, Lori Archer Raible, Samuel Son, and Charlotte Matthews—our fearless and vulnerable guide. I'm honored that "Spills" was named a semifinalist for the 2019 Alex Albright Creative Nonfiction Prize competition for the *North Carolina Literary Review.*

I originally wrote the following essays for the Mockingbird website: "Keepsake, Part 2," "Signs and Wonders," "My Most Selfish Prayer," "Comma, Love," and "I Sing Asa." Mockingbird Ministries is like *The Atlantic* with a provocative Christian slant, and I have admired the writing of David Zahl and C.J. Green from afar. It's a gift to receive their encouragement.

"Exposure" first appeared on the website of *The Good Men Project.* I hope to contribute more essays here, as I hope to live into the lifelong project of becoming a good man.

"A Gracious Plenty" was published by Gareth Higgins in *The Porch Magazine.* I'm touched that he would include my stories about my beloved mentors on his website devoted to "a slow conversation about beautiful & difficult things."

April Williams, we do not fear the rewrite! I'm so grateful for the time and energy you spent with this manuscript. Thank you for bringing your intelligence and insight gently between my words. Thank you for your gorgeous foreword and your daughter's artwork!

I readily acknowledge that writing is a self-centered act—especially when the piece is to be published. It takes an author's attention away from other priorities, like caring for one's family. So, I am most thankful to Ginny Taylor-Troutman for her loving support, which makes my dreams possible.

And thanks to you, gentle reader. It is always a grace to be read.

ABOUT THE AUTHOR

Andrew Taylor-Troutman is the poet pastor of Chapel in the Pines Presbyterian Church.

Andrew holds master's degrees from Union Presbyterian Seminary and the University of Virginia. He has previously authored *Take My Hand,* a theological memoir/sermon collection, *Parables of Parenthood,* a study of the parables of Jesus through the interpretative lens of family, and *Earning Innocence,* a novella in the form of a pastor's daily journal.

Andrew lives in Chapel Hill, North Carolina with his wife, who is also an ordained minister, and their three children.

www.facebook.com/ataylortroutman